Pequod Poems:
Gamming with *Moby-Dick*

Pequod Poems:
Gamming with *Moby-Dick*

Poems by

Wilda Morris

Cover artist: I.W. Tabor
Cover design by Shay Culligan

ISBN: 978-1-949229-60-8

Kelsay Books
Aldrich Press
www.kelsaybooks.com

Contents

Part V: Melville

Notes
About the Author

Dedication

This book is dedicated to the memory of Herman Melville,

to the memory of three of my teachers from Iowa City High School, to whom I wish I could give copies: Elizabeth Winbigler (English), Robert White (Civics) and Moretta Yearnd (history),

and to my husband, Edgar Morris,
with appreciation for his patience with my poetry, his willingness to drive to from Illinois to Massachusetts and back listening to *Moby-Dick* on CD all the way there and half the way back, but most of all, for years of love and support.

I want to express my appreciation to all my poet friends who critiqued individual poems or drafts of this book, especially to Lisken Van Pelt Dus, Caroline Johnson, Susan Moss, Barbara Eaton, Fereshteh Azad, Bakul Banerjee, Ruan Wright, Linda Wallen and Myron Stokes, as well as Justen Ahren (and peers at the residency on Martha's Vineyard), Robin Chapman (and participants in Poetry Camp at The Clearing in Ellison Bay, Wisconsin), Marilyn Taylor (and workshop participants at Björklunden in Bailey's Harbor, Wisconsin), the Illinois State Poetry Society (Lisle and Darien chapters), Poets & Patrons, the Arbor Hill Poetry Gang, San Miguel Poetry Week, Poetry Pilgrims, and Poetic Lights. Thank you, also, to Will Hansen (and The Newberry Library in Chicago), and to the staff at Panera on the east side of Bolingbrook for permitting me to hide out there to do much of my writing and revising.

Acknowledgments

The following poems have been previously published. In some cases, the poem has been revised and/or the title changed.

"Ahab Speaks of the Wind" – *Poets Online*
"Archy Reflects on His Life" – *The Basil O'Flaherty*
"Fire" – *Voices in the Wind*
"Ishmael Describes Weaving with Queequeg" – *The Basil O'Flaherty*
"Israel Reflects on the Try Works Fire" – *Pangolin Review*
"Ishmael Writes to a Friend Back Home" – *Prairie Light Review* (republished in *The Basil O'Flaherty*)
"It Wasn't a Mermaid" – *DuPage Valley Review*
"Lamenting Fate" – *The Basil O'Flaherty*
"Mary Starbuck's Letter" – *The Basil O'Flaherty*
"Melville in Love" – *Pangolin Review*
"Moon Dust" – *The Journal of Modern Poetry*
"Noah's Flood" – *Voices on the Wind* (republished in *The Weekly Avocet*)
"Phantom at Arrowhead" – *The Basil O'Flaherty*
"Reminder" – *Pangolin Review*
"Starbuck Ponders Fate and Free Will" – *The Basil O'Flaherty*
"The English Sailor's Lament" – *The Basil O'Flaherty*
"The Song of the Maltese Sailor" – *The Basil O'Flaherty*
"Tools" – *Lilipoh*
"Vagabond" – *The Kerf*
"White according to Ishmael" – *Unlost Journal*

Preface

A few years ago I decided to fill in gaps in my education created by the fact that I took no literature courses in college. I borrowed recordings of classics and listened to them while commuting. Intrigued by Herman Melville's language, quotablility and insights into human nature, I copied favorite lines from *Moby-Dick* and used them as inspiration for poems, thinking of them as "gams," similar to interactions between whaling ships at sea. I signed up for a class on *Moby-Dick* taught by Will Hansen, Curator of Americana at The Newberry Library in Chicago, and actually read the book for the first time. I learned that there has been a resurgence of interest in *Moby-Dick* during the past decade or so, resulting in an opera, a new musical, an award-winning play, artwork, novels and poetry.

A writer's residency on Martha's Vineyard sponsored by the Noepe Center for the Literary Arts provided impetus for writing more poems inspired by *Moby-Dick*, as did attendance at Poetry Camp at The Clearing in Door County, Wisconsin. I imagined back-stories of characters, wrote letters from wives to husbands on The Pequod, and thought about what the sinking of ship meant for Ahab's and Starbuck's sons, and for Ishmael's later life.

Melville used a number of literary genre in Moby-Dick so I used a variety of poetry forms. I tried to do justice to the characters, plot and themes of the novel, and to the troubled literary genius who wrote it. The Notes section identifies the forms (which sometimes create unusual line breaks), and in some cases provides additional information. Some of my poems may seem like digressions, but that is appropriate, I think, considering Melville's digressions in *Moby-Dick*.

Where an epigraph refers to a chapter, it is, of course, a chapter in *Moby-Dick*. I hope you enjoy the various ways I have played with and responded to Melville's great novel.

Wilda Morris   October 23, 2018

Part I: Pequod Poems

Ishmael in New Bedford: A Mesostic Poem

What a fine frosty night; how Orion glitters....
(Chapter 2)

Wind screams
along sullen **s**hore; strong cold gusts
blow clouds **an**d
scen**ts** of fish from New Bedford docks

raise ridges

of bubbles,
high as the top of a hull.
Now dusk drops.
I watch wav**es** wash the rocky land

and night **fi**ll
with calm **tr**anquility.
Orion the archer,
belted with light, **s**word
at hand, gleams
above a qua**y**.

Cold clutches me, **gn**aws my face,
wh**ip**s my arms,
grasps
my feet wit**h** icy claws.
I daydream I'm in Sumatra

far from **here**
rocking in gentle
swells under a sapphire sky.

17

O gentle
hunter, find me a place
to sleep tonight, lead me
to a lit fire, whiskey,
a bed with warm blankets.

After filigreed stars fade
and the sun is aloft,
I'll seek passage on a whaler,
but now, I walk under
Orion till I find
a place to stay
for one night,
then I'll make the sea my home.

Oceans

Observe ever-moving
open water. Orcas—
orphic omens—predict
our descent into deep
obscurity. But wait!
Osprey and cormorants
own the sky, teach us flight.

A Pequod Sailor Speaks

The Atlantic rolling onto the sandy shores
of Nantucket, piping plovers and screeching gulls,
oysters and crabs in the inlets,
rising sun painting pastel wrinkles
on ever-moving water—
this was nature as I loved it
in my boyhood.

Broken masts, bereft wives
and fatherless children
tell another story of the sea.
Still, I can't resist the challenge
to prove my manhood
and test my nature against
the earth's salty liquid overcoat.

At first it is easy.
We float through languid days
on indolent trade winds under skies
blue as Nantucket violets.
When I watch the sun set, coloring
the infinite spread of fluid ribbons,
I drift into meditative silence.

Sudden winds bellow, curdle foam.
Sword-sharp, they rip the sails, shriek
and break the mast. Lightning stabs
billowing water. The ocean I love bares its teeth,
opens its jaws, eager to swallow ship and crew.
The turncoat sea leaps over the bulwarks,
Judas, kissing the captain.

The Three Mates Speak of Aunt Charity

Stubb:
Aunt Charity's kind and convivial, jolly like me,
but odd. I laughed when she brought on board
that one jar of pickles she'd canned,
as if it were plenty for a three-year passage.

Flask:
The old lady tucked copies of Watts in every
seaman's hammock. Does she think they sing
God Our Help in Ages Past to pass the long nights
or while chasing whales?

Starbuck:
I'm glad she doesn't know the sailors compete
to kick those hymnbooks farthest down the deck.
Aunt Charity was kind to bring me extra quills
to keep the log books, but didn't think of ink.

Stubb:
The worst mistake was that ginger-jup tea
she gave the steward for the harpooneers.
What the devil, I thought, when I smelled that stuff,
it's no way to warm the fire of a shivering cannibal!
The sea drank it willingly when I tossed it out,
but a cold, exhausted man needs something stronger.

Flask:
When she came on board
with the long oil-ladle in one hand,
a whale lance in the other,
she looked like a comical queen.
What strange staff and scepter!

Stubb:
Last time she bustled aboard,
she brought a Bible for Dough-Boy,
though I don't think he can read,
and a welcome night-cap for me.
Aye, the name Charity suits her—
in her own curious way.

The Captain

Ahab
answers to nobody. Bold, he never
bothers to check with the mates or
crew, demands
devotion. Egotistical,
evil in intent, feudal and
fatalist, ungodly but godlike. Once
gone to sea, he has no boss.
He says, I, and
I alone, judge what to do, then we
jump. One king for a
kingdom, one leader, Captain Ahab, is
lord of the ship. Monomaniacal, he searches only for
Moby Dick, will not be satisfied until
nothing remains of the white whale, the
one that bit off his leg, put him in agony. He
paces the deck, quickly stifles
quarrels, rationalizes his
resolve to slaughter that
sea creature, take the life of
the animal he hates. He'll use any means to
utterly destroy it. Vengeful and
vicious, he seeks the whale, is
willing to expose the crew to
extermination, devote years to his impious mission. The crew
yields to his will, zombie-like and
zealous.

Ahab Speaks of the Wind

(Chapter 135)

A vile wind blown
through prison cells
and wards of hospitals
now comes
innocent as fleeces—tainted.

Were I the wind,
I'd blow no more
on such a wicked world.
I'd crawl to a cave
and slink there.

The wind!
Who ever conquered it?
Run tilting at it
and you but run through it—
a coward wind
will not stand
to receive a single blow.

Cunning.
Malicious.

And yet
there's something
glorious and gracious
in the wind.

Blow my keeled soul along!

White according to Ishmael

(Chapter 42)

the whiteness of the whale
appalled me

whiteness   enhances beauty
in   marbles   pearls
snow-white charger
ermine

there yet lurks an elusive something
which strikes   panic to the soul

white bear of the poles
irresponsible ferociousness
in the fleece of celestial innocence

white shark
gliding ghostliness

albatross
unspotted whiteness
with a hooked, Roman bill
vast archangel wings

pallor of the dead
the shroud
ghosts rising in a milk-white fog

the visible absence of color
the concrete of all colors
blankness

of all these things
the Albino whale was the symbol

Skin, Clothes – Ishmael Shares What He Learned

Beginning with a line from Chapter 3

A man can be honest in any sort of skin.
In any kind of clothes he can be stingy,
tyrannical, despotic and monomaniacal.
You can't judge character by looks.

In any kind of clothes, he can be stingy
as Bildad signing sailors to work on the Pequod
for the least pay possible, or

tyrannical, despotic, monomaniacal,
obsessed as Ahab, focused on revenge
for some experienced or sensed slight.

You can't judge character by looks—
tattoos, matted hair, dirty coat, dark skin—
Queequeg was like a brother to me.

Pip's Secret Thoughts

Even here at sea, I carry with me
the scent of turnip greens,
the taste of chitlins Auntie soaked
and simmered. I hear music
pour through an open chapel door:
Steal Away, Jacob's Ladder,
Swing Low, Sweet Chariot.
I see Maggie dancin' on the village green,
dark braids bouncin' on her back,
her skirt a swirl of red and yellow.
All these I hide as I shake my tambourine
to please the crew. I pray the gods
will be kind to this little black boy
and bring me safely home.

Sailors' Dreams on the Pequod

The sailors sigh for Polynesian girls
or for the wives or fiancées they've left
back home decked out in lacy gowns and pearls,
hair spilling from their bonnets in soft curls,
but when they reach for them they are bereft.

Long months at sea these curvy specters haunt
with beauty daytime eyes can never see,
and all the loveliness those women flaunt
seems to the mariners a cruel taunt,
and every kiss an unreality.

The tangled blankets they are twisting in
when called to watch for whales another day
are damp with sweat, but there is no soft skin
for all delights of night just fade away.

Mary Starbuck's Letter

April 25th, Dear Husband, Each day our
Boy eats his porridge, then insists I take him to the
crest of the Hill to look for the Pequod's sails. He
drops his toy ship & jumps up & down
each time he sees a Mast, sure his
father has returned. While you're at sea, he
grows so fast—he's learned much & now asks to
hear the fates of Captains & first mates. He's 2
inches taller than when you left & says he will
join a whaling crew when he's a man so he can
kill Whales just like his papa. Every night we reread the
letter The Bachelor delivered. I'll endeavor to start
my garden plot before the weather's hot.
Nothing fills the time so well as to plant & weed
onions, potatoes, corn & lettuce seed. The beach
plum's in bud & the birds are no longer
quiet, so I know 'tis spring. Piping plovers
ran across the sand above the tideline today. I
sent Maid to buy Sea Beans & cod. She cooked chowder
tonight. Our Boy had a headache. He was
unhappy and ate little. When I put him to bed, I told him your
voyage should end soon. I went outside so I could listen to
waves and see the lighthouse. I so want to know
'xactly where in the ocean you are, Husband, & when
you're coming back. I pray that before the rockrose blooms a
Zephyr will bring you safely home. Your loving wife, Mary

Letter to Capt. Ahab from His Wife

Please write to me, my husband dear
and tell me if you're well. I fear
your missing leg still gives you pain,
your haunting headaches still remain
and have become much more severe.

You have been gone at least two years.
No letters come to bring me cheer
and though I never should complain—
please write to me.

I look to Sea and hope you're near
but sometimes dream you disappear
in sullen waves or hurricane.
Not knowing causes so much strain
that I can't help but shed a tear.
Please write to me.

Fire

Aye, I widowed that poor girl when I married her.
~Ahab (Chapter 132)

Just one night of passion
before I sailed, leaving my young wife,
our one son beginning to grow
in the hold of her ship,
harvested before I returned
with the Pequod's hold full of spermaceti.

Dismasted by Moby Dick,
dismembered and unmanned
by the pierce of shattered ivory,
I walk the deck on one foot
and one limb crafted by the carpenter.
Only vengeance keeps me afloat
in this cruel world
where neither my widowed mother's god
nor Fedallah's god of fire
can repair my broken sail,
my leaky hold,

where no god can return to me
the fire of my marriage bed.

Archy Reflects on His Life

1.

Sent by Mother to collect blue mussels from tide pools,
I'd squat on rocks, peer into the watery garden,
wish I were small enough to swim
among pebbles, periwinkle snails and plankton.
Sea anemones shrank into small blobs
when I ruffled their tentacles with a twig.
I touched the stick to spiny sea urchins,
laughed as they pointed quills at me
and called them *poor little porcupines.*
I examined dog whelks, picked up starfish,
flipped them over in my hand and imagined
their stories before I turned to clusters of mussels,
filled my wicker basket and headed home,
taking the mysteries of the sea with me.

2.

On Saturdays in the parlor, my sisters sat up straight
on the settee, proud of flowers, scripture verses,
alphabet and numbers stitched across their samplers.
Big brother Johnny and I ran out the door and down
to the docks, watched carts bring provisions to outgoing vessels
while incoming whalers unloaded barrels of oil. We admired
sun-leathered men high in the masts or spilling
off ships into the city, heading for homes, bawdy houses
or bars. We climbed linden trees, pretended to stand watch
in a crow's nest as we looked out over the water.
Many evenings, by the light of sperm-oil lamps,
we read tales of adventure on the sea.
We pricked our fingers, signed a blood oath to sail
together someday to search the ocean for sperm whales.

3.

I miss those days when we were young and fearless.
I miss Johnny's jokes, his teasing and how we raced each other
up the rigging to watch for whales. Now Johnny's home
with consumption. I wonder what he would say
of Ahab, our half-mad captain. We all took oaths
to wreak vengeance on the cursed creature he hates,
the white whale that took his leg. When I lie in my hammock
trying to sleep, I can't help counting omens:
typhoon, lightning, three masts lit like candles,
compass needle turned backward, moaning mermaids,
a sailor falling into the sea, lifebuoy sinking,
black hawk swiping the captain's hat. I fear
I will never see Johnny again, never again gather mussels
for Mother from the tide pools of Nantucket.

Ishmael Writes to a Friend Back Home

Better sleep with a sober cannibal than a drunken
Christian.

~Ishmael (Chapter 3)

Depressed with life on land, I thought it better
to head for Nantucket and set sail, rather than sleep-
walk through another winter. I left home alone with
meager possessions. In New Bedford, I met a
harpooneer. An experienced whaler, sober
and strong, Queequeg was a cannibal,
but so congenial—more like a brother than
a friend. His mistake—trusting me to select a
ship. I picked the Pequod, whose captain was drunken
with vengeance, having few values I'd call Christian.

The Song of the Maltese Sailor

Now would all the waves were women, then I'd go drown,
and chassee with them evermore!
~Maltese sailor (Chapter 40)

If all the waves were women
I'd happily drown and chassee forever.
I'd glide through sensuous oceans
with my wild and willing partners.

I'd drown and happily dance forever
between the fishes and the kelp
with those waves, those willing women
sliding, gliding and caressing.

I'd bow to the fishes, sea birds and kelp.
Caught in each voluptuous swell,
sliding and gliding, I'd sashay
to the rhythm of the dance.

A voluptuous swell would waltz me off,
hug me, kiss me and caress me
as I glided to the vibrant rhythm
of the ocean's pulsing dance.

The waves would all embrace me.
I'd glide through sensuous oceans, moving
to the rhythm of the ocean's dance.
I'd happily drown, if all the waves were women.

The Steward's Story

I'm stuck on this ship with sailors who laugh
at my pudgy cheeks, pinch 'em and call me Dough-Boy.
I never learned to read or do much 'rithmetic.
Father, broke and beaten down when his bakery failed,
signed me up for the Pequod. Room and grub
for three years, they said, and the 280th lay.
The cook tells me that's half what most stewards get,
but Father's happy with one less mouth to feed.

When we set sail, I feared wind and water,
but now it's mostly men making me miserable.
When cook sends me to serve the harpooneers,
Queequeg snaps his big white fangs, says he'll gnaw
my arm. Tashtego darts me like a whale with his fork.
Daggoo once shoved my head in a trencher, held me down
while Tash dragged his knife around my head
as if to take my scalp. They like to hear me squeal.

I slink into the pantry, watch through slats
till those demons are done with dinner.
They call me back, complaining of tainted meat
or roaches in the molasses pot, threaten to pick my bones
or throw me to the sharks. My hands shake an' I stumble
over my feet. I fear 'em more than typhoons,
more than I fear Captain Ahab or that white whale
he's sworn to kill. God, how I want to go home!

Ishmael Describes Weaving with Queequeg

(Chapter 47)

I kept   passing and repassing
the   woof
between   long yarns of the warp,
my own hand   the shuttle

Queequeg   slid his   sword
between the threads
carelessly
unthinkingly drove home every yarn

it seemed
the Loom of Time
and I myself
weaving away at the Fates

fixed threads of the warp
              necessity

I   weave my own destiny
into these unalterable threads

Queequeg's   indifferent sword
hitting the woof
slantingly
   crookedly
      strongly
         weakly
producing   contrast
shapes and fashions   warp and woof
         this   must be chance

aye, chance, free will,
and necessity
interweavingly working together

chance
has the last   blow

Poor Pip,

Ending with a line from Chapter 93

little black boy in a place and time where white masters
expected little black boys to work dawn to dusk, to serve,
to bow to superiors, to step off the sidewalk
and let the white folk pass, when little black boys
were supposed to be happy with their plight, to sing and play
the tambourine all night and rise to work another day.

Poor Pip, did you sign on to the Pequod because you ran
from a harsh master or just for adventure, thinking as cabin boy
you'd find freedom, get to see a wider world across the water?
How were you to know you'd be called to substitute
with Stubb's crew, to pull an oar while Tash harpooned a whale?

You never dreamed you'd end up in the ocean,
tangled in strangling rope till Tash cut you and the beast free,
and Stubb would curse you, tell you the oil from the creature
cut from the line was worth far more than you
in an Alabama market where poor little black boys are sold,
declaring he wouldn't save you if you jumped again.

Pip, when courage failed you a second time, bounced you
from the boat, did you feel you'd lost the last thread
of whatever free will life gave a poor black boy like you?
When you floated away from the disappearing boat,
did you know you were knotted in the threads of fate?
As you sank into the deep, then rose, your bobbing head hardly
more than a peppercorn in the boundless circle of sea and sky,
was it some vast indifference you glimpsed as you
saw God's foot upon the treadle of the loom?

Stubb's Remorse

With a repeated line quoted from Chapter 99

Pip's been crazy since he jumped a second time
from my whaleboat. I'd told him if he leaped again
I'd not risk losing a whale for the likes of him,
who'd fetch much less in an Alabama market
than the spermaceti of one beast in New Bedford.

Would he had died, or I.

I didn't intend to follow through on my threat,
didn't mean to leave Pip bobbing on the ocean,
floating so far he could no longer see the ship
or our boat, but my face was turned toward the winged whale
while the cabin boy floated away. I figured
Starbuck or Flask would pluck him from the sea.

Would he had died, or I.

I can't bear to see the delusional boy roam the deck,
asking if anyone has seen that coward Pip.
When at last he was pulled back into the Pequod,
he left something of himself in the water.
Ishmael says Pip learned the gods are callous
and unkind and that's what left him mad.

Would he had died, or I.

Each day, I hear the little black boy babbling,
mumbling, berating his lost self,
He repeats what I taught him, that one
who jumps from a whaleboat is a coward,
and pastes that label on himself.
It sickens me to see what he's become.

Would he had died, or I.

Now Ahab's taken him under his wing,
two crazies walking the deck together
or heading down to the captain's quarters.
Now we're on the whaling ground,
Old Ahab is determined to fight the white whale.
I fear my wish may soon come true—

I will die, and so will Pip.

Starbuck Ponders Fate and Free Will

I heard the old man mutter that he must,
as always, play the cards he's given by fate.
He's moody, lunatic, unhinged, and cursed.

He stalks across the deck so full of hate,
is not dissuaded by the shrieking gale.
The sharks will gather round, we'll all be bait

if that white whale strikes at us with his tail.
Old Ahab thinks his destiny is near—
to kill the source of evil. If he fail,

the sea will bury us, the sky will clear
with nothing left to show that we exist.
Why won't he turn, and why has he no fear?

What is it makes his wild emotions twist,
refusing to forgo the unholy tryst?

It Wasn't a Mermaid

. . . Whether it was a reality or a dream, I could never entirely settle.

~Ishmael (chapter 4)

I never know for sure if it was real
or did I dream I swam once with a seal
whose half-articulated wailing cry
was ghost-like, haunting all the Pequod's crew.
She sought the pup she lost in days gone by.
Is this a memory I can't construe
or did I dream I swam once with a seal?
I never know for sure if it was real.

Stubb and the Cook

Italicized words quoted from Chapter 64.

They call him Cook.
They call him Ebony.
They call him old Fleece.

Stubb, the second mate, calls him
from his hammock near midnight
to grill him a whale steak,
no matter that the cook has to rise
before sunup to prepare food
for the crew.

Stubb may think he is kind
when he orders the cook
to taste the perfectly-prepared steak
while complaining it's too tender.

Stubb asks, *Where were you born, cook?*
And *Where do you expect to go to?*
not to touch the old man's humanity
but to tease and belittle.

Stubb tells the cook he can go,
calls him to return,
orders him to quiet the sharks
slapping their tails against the ship,
swarming around a dead whale,
smacking their lips as they feast on its fatness.
Stubb commands him to preach to the critters,
not for the good of the sharks
but for his own entertainment.

Stubb hears the cook tell the sharks
to stop the damn racket they make
while filling their damn bellies,
says, *Cook! why, damn your eyes,*
you mustn't swear that way
when you're preaching.

The cook speaks wisdom
when he tells the sharks all he can ask
of them is to govern their sharkishness.
Stubb doesn't hear condemnation
of his own sharkish behavior.

As the cook limps back to his hammock
he mumbles, *Wish, by gor! whale eat him,*
'stead of him eat whale. I'm bressed
if he ain't more of shark dan Massa Shark hisself.
Stubb does not hear.

Oranges

Now as the blubber envelopes the whale precisely as the rind does an orange, so is it stripped off from the body precisely as an orange is sometimes stripped by spiralizing it.

(Chapter 67)

It's easy to sit on the deck,
strip from the orb in your hand
spirals of golden rind.

Sweet juice dampens your palms,
decorates your beard,
drips from your chin.

As for stripping whale blubber,
nearly-naked men spiralizer it
as the windlass rolls the body

over and over in the salty sea.
Hooked and raised in the air, the blubber
drips blood on water, deck, and sailors.

Oranges brought on board are gone
well before the ship sails into the Sea of Japan
where sperm whales breach,

where blubber is cooked down,
squeezed and stored in barrels
for the long trip home.

Ishmael Reflects on the Try-Works Fire

Beginning with a line from Chapter 96

Look not too long in the face of the fire—
those forking flames are a devilish sight.
The blaze hypnotizes as it grows higher;
it blinds your eyes to the sun's true light.

I'll never believe what I've been taught
by my frowning mother, that all men fell
and my soul is damned—in the flames I'm caught.
She said, *Go to church, or you'll go to hell*.

Instead of the fire with guilt and dread,
turn to the wisdom of Solomon's book
or the Man of Sorrows, the life he led—
he spread compassion with his gentle look.

How different would be my mother's face
if her theology reflected grace.

What If?

Is Ahab, Ahab?
~Ahab (Chapter 132)

If Ahab brought a puppy
aboard the Pequod, its wagging tail
would be more comfort than a pipe.

If Ahab had a kitten
it would pounce on a loose thread
from Ahab's typhoon-torn coat.

If he had a puppy
it would patrol the deck,
running along beside him, running ahead.

If he had a kitten
it would curl up on his lap
as he studied each chart and map.

If he had a puppy,
it would lick and rub against his remaining leg,
reminding him he still had one.

If Ahab cuddled a kitten,
in its eyes he would see
the yearning eyes of his young wife.

If Ahab petted a puppy with soft brown fur
he might dream of tousling his son's hair again
instead of the wild pursuit of the white whale.

Prayer of the First Mate

Mysterious, ever-moving
ocean God,
maker of dolphins
that bob and play
around the ship,
creator of sperm whales
whose oil lights our lamps,
and of the sharks
who feed on the blood
and bodies of our catch,

mysterious, decisive
ocean God
who alone determines
the length of each island,
the depth and breadth of each sea,
whose Son stood
in a storm-spun fishing boat,
calming the water,

mysterious, unfathomable
ocean God,
who created mankind
in your own image,
where is your image in Ahab
who for vengeance
would sacrifice not just himself
but a whole crew of men
made in your image?
Where is that image in me—
I who have not the courage
to contest Ahab's evil intent?

Mysterious, invisible
ocean God,

if you cannot show yourself,
at least show me a sign
you hold us safely
under the wings
of the red-billed sea-hawk.

The English Sailor's Lament

We are the lads to hunt him up his whale!
~English sailor (Chapter 40)

He is the man whose face is mysterious,
the man with one ivory leg.
He is the man who paces the deck
while plotting his vengeance.

We are the lads who seek great adventure,
the boys out searching for whales.
We are the lads who are testing our manhood
against all that is wild.

He is the man the white whale unmasted,
the captain whose moods we all fear.
He is the man sworn wholly to vengeance
against the white whale.

We are the lads vowed to hunt for his foe,
who drank to his need for revenge.
We are the men who give our wills over
to the will of our captain.

We are the crew who'll be drowned in the ocean,
whose wives will be widowed, forlorn.
We are the lads who will leave orphaned children,
when we make the seabed our home.

Ahab's Harpoon

With phrases quoted from Chapters 113, 126, 16, and 36

To gain the strength of twelve tribes or twelve disciples,
twelve rods heated, pulled and pounded
in hell-hot heat on the anvil. Forged not with prayer
but from the good-luck charm of broken horseshoe nails,
half-melted magic twisted into one iron
as red-orange flames blazed and infernal sparks flew.

The unkempt captain's steel razors forged into barbs
sharp as the needle-sleet of the Icy Sea,
strong and keen-edged as the upper mandible
of the albatross, sharper than the blade
of Queequeg's tomahawk, welded to the shank
by Perth—the Promethean scarred and suffering
servant of Ahab—barbs tempered and baptized in the blood
of the trinity of *pagan harpooneers*
not in the name of the Father, but *in nomine diaboli.*

The iron fitted to a hickory pole
and a long strand of tow-line, twisted and braided,
secured in the socket, the Three Fates,
that trinity of iron, pole and rope,
and Ahab, the *grand, ungodly, godlike man*
who would *strike the sun* if it insulted him
confident he will kill the white whale.

White

White is ominous in
whales, like tempestuous
wind and breakers, the spun
water that the white whale
whipped into a fury
when the harpoon struck him.
What did Ahab expect?

The White Whale Likens Himself to
the Doubloon

Each man on the Pequod sees me in his own way.

Queequeg, whose life was corkscrewed
by the cultures he experienced,
remembers me for the twisted harpoons
wrenched in my back.

For Stubb, I am the promise of a juicy steak
cut by Dagoo, grilled to his liking,
and as a chance to rankle the black cook,
to laugh again at a defenseless old man.

Starbuck says I am a dumb beast,
doing what is natural to me
as whaling to him, says it is blasphemous
to seek me for revenge. For him,
I am the hope of a cask of sweet-smelling sperm oil
to satisfy investors in Nantucket.

Fedallah thinks of me as fulfillment
of prophecy, darkness and doom
for himself and the captain—
whose fate is tied inexorably to his own.

To Ishmael, I am sorcerous, supernatural, spectral,
demonic, a shroud-like symbol of death.
Whiteness separated from beauty, innocence, spiritual power
is a source of dread, a challenge that casts on him
a magic spell, a desire to chase and kill me.
I am a legend, a paradox as imponderable as himself.

Ahab, the vengeful one, sees me
as embodiment of evil, not realizing
he looks in a mirror when he looks at me.

Little Pip plays his tambourine, tightens
ropes, cleans the deck, never saying
what he thinks of me.

Stubb Ponders Shadow and Substance

Methinks we have hugely mistaken this matter of Life and Death. Methinks
that what they call my shadow here on earth is my true substance.

~Ishmael (Chapter 7)

I don't understand the substance
of Ishmael's argument here,
but what does it matter?
What he says may be true.
In the end, each of us is heading for death.
We will become ashes or dust, ghost or shadow.

But I'm jolly, pay no attention to shadow.
What I eat becomes my substance.
I laugh at danger, don't concern myself with death.
I don't fret about what I see and hear,
don't worry if dire predictions are true.
When I die, I'll cease to matter.

For now, it's a matter
of chasing the shadow
of a white whale. True,
he bit off Ahab's leg, but not his substance.
Ahab is still here;
he did not succumb to death.

Like me, the captain defies death.
For that monomaniac, there is no matter
as important as harpooning that whale here
in the Sea of Japan. It casts a constant shadow
on Ahab, on his spirit and his substance.
The whole crew knows that's true.

I think I am closer to what is true
for me if I laugh in the presence of death.
This was always my substance.
Perhaps that's really the root of the matter—
my wanting to be fearless in the valley of the shadow
the Psalmist speaks of, wanting to be fearless here

when the Angel of Death knocks and I hear
the window of my life closing, when it's true
that what I want more than safety is Nantucket cherries. A shadow
crosses the deck. I try to be bold, look into the face of death.
I try to be jolly, but this is not a laughing matter;
it really is a question of substance.

So here I flail, my substance, the me that is here,
the me composed of matter, asking if Ishmael's thought is true.
Will part of me survive death? Is what you see just my shadow?

Cherries

. . . cherries! cherries! cherries! Oh, Flask, for one red cherry ere we die!
~Stubb (Chapter 135)

One red cherry.
One more walk on the cobblestones of Sunset Hill Road
past the old saltbox houses.
One more sight of Sankaty Head Light,
its beams reflected on the water.
One more big bowl of clam chowder.
One more race with my brother in thick morning fog.
One picnic on the beach as the sun sets.
One last morning, sun rising through purple clouds
over the Atlantic as gulls fill the air with shrieks and acrobatics,
as piping plovers and semipalmated sandpipers scavenge the shore,
time slow as horseshoe crabs crawling in the sand.
One red cherry from a Nantucket tree before I die.

Prophecy

I now prophesy that I will dismember my dismemberer.
~Ahab (Chapter 37)

Ahab is another Icarus,
ignoring all warnings:
the prophecies of Elijah and Gabriel,
the albatross,
the spirit-spout that led us on night after night—
disappearing and reappearing—
the seldom-seen specter
of the great white squid,
the letter to the dead mate of The Jeroboam
falling into the waves,
lightning turning the needle of the compass,
the ambiguity of Fedallah's words . . . .

What he reads as promise
of triumph over the white whale
falls like Icarus on his melted wings,
sinks to the seabed with ship and crew.

Part II: Aftermath

Sonnet 80 Suite

Movement 1: Ishmael Remembers

I used to weep when I sat down to write
of my adventures, knowing I must name
the captain of the ship, that man of might
whose hubris doomed his crew and brought him fame
or rather infamy, for Ahab is
reviled by those whose wives and children bear
the burdens grief lay down, results of his
obsession, Moby Dick. It would appear
the captain thought we could remain afloat
although that great white whale gave us a ride.
He knew the whale would fight, would pull our boat,
but didn't fathom in his haughty pride
leviathan would turn to drive the ship away
crush it, bring on disaster and decay.

Movement 2: Four & 's

Proudest – A Sailor's Unspoken Apology

Pip, truly I'm not proud
of how the crew treated you like a pest
worth less than a wisp of dust,
how often we greeted you with sour
looks, were often rude
as you scrubbed the deck we trod.
We considered you like mold or rust.
How did you feel when we'd prod
you to play your tambourine? Though dour,
you shook those jingles off as we strode
the deck and danced until we'd drop.

Tongue-Tied – Queequeg's Thoughts as Interpreted
   by Ishmael

My father was a king, kept Rokovoko united
behind our traditions. When foreign ships sailed in, I noted
how different their clothes, habits and religion. I tuned
my ears to hear and asked a mariner to guide
my understanding. One day, I sailed out into
the wider world and learned each tenet
Christians taught, but saw how sailors acted when the tide
took us to port. Better stay with the faith Father touted.
I'm unfit to be prince or high priest, by dint
of habits I've learned all these years that I've been gone.
Does Father still wonder where I am, what I'm doing?

Soundless – Starbuck Ponders

While the sinking Pequod sounds
the sea, I sound my soul,
its clamoring a loud
racket I try to silence. I send
myself messages, try to undo
my distress, provide myself a dose
of hope and faith. But fear, like a sled
on ice, slips back in. I lose
confidence that God will lend
me aid, wonder what lesson
I should still learn before my life is done.

Shallowest – Ahab Speaks

I've known forty years of privation, sweat
and peril on the lonely, often lethal
sea, where waves swell and winds howl,
my face leathered by tropical sun and salt.
My young wife gathers shells
along the shore. My only son washes
his bare feet in waves while fearing I'm lost.
On my marriage bed, I left but one shallow
dent. I sailed first for adventure, then for wealth,
now for vengeance against that great white whale.
Will I make it home? Will I ever be whole?

Movement 3: Ishmael to Queequeg

I praise you, O humble spirit,
your name, your worth.
your help.
Deep in the wide ocean, thrive.
The worst was this: my love
was your decay.

Movement 4: Finale From Ishmael Who Survived Erasure

                        wide   the ocean
            the
      bark

      wreck'd,   a worthless boat,

          and I   cast away

Lament of Queequeg's Father as Translated by an American Sea Captain

Where is my eldest son? Has he returned?
Each day I pray a ship will come to shore
and bring Queequeg. I hear the breakers roar
and wonder what he's done and what he's learned.

Queequeg could be king. I'd step aside
and let him rule in Rokovoko. He
was born to be a king, rule after me.
He doesn't have to wait until I've died.

For days when first he went to sea alone
his mother cried aloud, would howl and shriek
and pull her hair. Our deity was weak
and did not hear, so nothing brought him home.

Where is my eldest son? Has he not returned?
He said he'd come back home someday. He swore
to tell us what he'd done and what he'd learned.

Sometimes I ask myself, Was his ship blown
away or sunk? He said he'd leave to seek
the wisdom of the West, learn their critique
of Rokovoko as a stepping stone

to better rule as king. Perhaps he lied.
I dream that he is dead, embalmed, that he
now floats in a war-wood canoe at sea,
and we won't meet again until I've died.

Where are you, Queequeg? Have you not returned?
My life is almost done and I abhor
your absence here. Come now, my son; you swore
to tell me what you've done and what you've learned.

Notes to Cabaco Found in a Box that Floated to Shore

December 21
Nantucket

I like the way you danced last night
and gave me a shiny ducat.
Don't forget to call on me
when you come back to Nantucket.
                              Elizabeth

Jan. 10
Lima, Peru

The weather's warm. The stars are bright.
The bar is open every night.
Come back to Lima where I dream of you
although I wonder if your love is true.
                              Your dark-eyed girl

July 17
Manilla

You know I don't want you to go.
I'll always be your Filipino girl
if you'll always be my best beau.
Any gal takes a risk when she loves
a wandering sailor like you—
can I trust you'll be faithful and true?
                              Carmen

July 21
Manilla

I'll cheer when your ship sails from the bay
now I know what all the girls say.
They've seen you on the river bridge
kissing that trollop named Midge.
On Calle Escolata
they saw you with Carlotta.
You were seen twice by the watchtower
giving some new girl a flower.
Goodbye. Please don't return.
                    Carmen

Ishmael Reflects on Fedallah

That tall, swarthy clairvoyant, dressed in black
except his braided-hair turban, whiter than the white whale,
the Parsee was always a shadow on the deck,
a muffled mystery, a frustrating puzzle
I still can't figure out.

A strange and secretive soothsayer,
a prophet who hissed when he spoke,
still he took to the boat when a whale was spied.
Harpoon in hand, he joined Ahab in the fray,
braved the spray, the turbulent water,
the teeth of the whale, as sharp and white
as Fedallah's one front tooth.

Almost mute, often motionless,
for hours as he surveyed the sea,
he sometimes seemed to sneer at Ahab,
to whom he was tied with invisible threads
or some imperceptible monkey rope.
Aye, they were woven together
as woof and warp, cursed with one curse.

Was he the devil with his tail coiled
inside his trousers as Stubb and Flask told
each other, the Prince of Darkness,
Beelzebub come with brimstone and fire
to bring down Ahab? He certainly seemed
a phantom from another world,
a demon consorting with humanity.
Was he just another shallow man, victim
like the rest of the crew of Ahab's hubris?

Were he and Ahab destined for the day
they met Moby Dick? Did some higher power
plot against them, pull the strings of fate?
It's still an ethereal enigma, a riddle
that shadows me as Fedallah shadowed the deck.

The Lament of Starbuck's Son

Mother says my father
was a brave man,
a hero of the whale fishery,
but to me he is absence,
emptiness.

Mother says my father
was kind,
a tender, loving man,
but to me he is heartbreak,
Mother's tears, her loneliness.

Mother says my father
was pious,
a faithful, believing man
but to me, he is a question—
why a loving God lets a father drown.

Mother says my father
was handsome, wind-tanned,
a well-remembered man
but to me he is a fading memory
and ongoing silence.

Ishmael, at the Golden Inn in Lima,
Remembers the Manxman

Yes, gentlemen, we called the Manxman Grizzle,
Greybeard, Geezer—he was the oldest mariner
on the Pequod, and most the superstitious.
As a lad on the Isle of Man in the Irish Sea
he learned of fairies, malevolent spirits
and shape-shifters. Always alert to omens,
he cursed the day he signed onto the doomed ship.
No sailor dared contradict when the old salt swore
Ahab was born with that lightning-shaped scar
down his face and neck, insisted it continued
all the way to the toes on his remaining foot.
No, Don Pedro, I can't say if that was true—Ahab
was never laid out and wrapped in a winding sheet.

When sailors insisted mermaids were moaning
below the bowsprit, the old Manxman convinced
the crew the wails—ghastly as the cries
of Herod's murdered Innocents—were not mermaids,
but the cries of the newly drowned, the plaintive pleas
of the vanished crew from The Rachel's whale boat,
carried into the deep by Moby Dick.

In the morning, Ahab averred what we had heard
in the darkness were but the mournful, melancholy cries
of young seals and their nursing mothers separated
in turbulent water. Don Pedro, I don't know why,
but it's the Manxman I believed.

Elijah Runs into Ishmael When He Returns to Nantucket

Told ye so! Old Thunder—
he's gone down with the ship
jus' like I said he would.
Made ye jump, Old Thunder did.
He never told ye what happened
off Cape Horn long ago. Never
told ye about the silver calabash
he spat in. Only told ye about his leg,
about how that parmacetti bit it off.
Didn't tell ye all the damage done
to him. Or about the prophecy, did he?

You mocked me,
said I spoke gibberish.
Wish ye and your sailor friends had listened,
but then, what was signed was signed,
names already on the list.
It was fixed and arranged a'ready by the heavens.
God pity all 'at's gone down to the depths.
God have mercy on their souls,
if they had any. Evening to ye.

Captain Gardiner Speaks

I am a harpooned whale, bleeding hate
at each sight of Ahab's son on a Nantucket street,
reminded, as I am, of the captain's refusal to square the yards,
join The Rachel's search for my young son
and the others in the boat the white whale towed
beyond the horizon after they darted him.

I hear Ahab's staccato voice, cold,
mechanical, a hammer striking the anvil
of my heart. *Don't touch a rope, mates!*
Captain Gardiner, I will not do it!

Ahab muttered a wish to forgive himself,
but dared not plead for my pardon.
He resumed his unholy mission
as my son vanished in a watery hell.

Now Ahab's fatherless son is twelve,
as old as mine when the sea consumed him,
wounded and wild, as icy as the old captain was.
He strides toward the harbor, ready
to sign on to a whaling ship, determined
to avenge his vengeful father.

The vicious leviathan will leave Ahab's widow childless.
I'll no longer be haunted by this image
of the heartless captain on the streets of Nantucket.

Ishmael Tells His Son of the Dangers of Whaling

All hands on deck, we pulled down sails,
lashed whale boats more tightly to the sides,
bailed out water as lightning slashed the sky
and winds wracked the ship, threatening
to tip us into Davy Jones' locker. The winds shrieked
and pounced like angry lions. Thunder growled
and crashed like cymbals. I struggled to stand upright,
to keep the tiller straight, steering into oncoming waves
as Poseidon roiled the sea, stirred clouds
into a torrential downpour. Or was it Tawhiri,
Polynesian god of storms, who rocked us,
tried to pull us into the vortex?
The gale knocked me to the floor.
Water rose like walls, slammed down on us.
Death stared me in the face as darkness
was sliced again by light. I was alert,
every part of me alive in the threatening night.

More dangerous, though, were the long days
of sunlight and warm breezes. From the rigging
I watched for whales until lulled into listlessness
and languor. Thoughts flowed into my mind,
passing through like the gentle waves.
My head emptied into hypnotic daydreams.
My eyes glazed like the sea. Time and again
I almost lost my grip and slipped from the rope.
I would have left but a few bubbles
in the calm surface as I fell through.

Part III: Memos to Herman Melville

Boundaries

Beginning with three lines by Lisel Mueller

The careful boundaries we draw and erase,
and always, around the edges,
the opaque wash of blue—
you knew these boundaries well
from your childhood with a stern mother
who ordered her children to sit, silent
and motionless, each afternoon as she napped,
demanded regular church attendance
and strict submission to every command.

You chafed, too, at the boundaries of obedience
on a whaler where labor was hard
and the captain so tyrannical that few
of the crew completed the voyage. You jumped ship
in the Marquesas where Victorian standards
of polite society were erased, freely enjoyed
the company of naked-breasted women
and questioned the supremacy of your parents' faith.

Yet you returned, made a proper marriage
to a judge's daughter. Though you sometimes
remembered those days in the south seas
with a sigh, quoting to yourself the lines by the Pope:
A very heathen in the carnal part
Yet still a sad good Christian at the heart,
you sheltered your austere and disapproving mother
in your household for years. The boundaries set
for good sons, husbands, and fathers
hung like a noose around your neck.

Sometimes you loosened the rope a bit
by meeting male friends in the barn
where you could smoke, share bawdy tales
and toss back ale without a woman's reprimand.

Did you find some peace in forbidding
entrance to your study as you wrote,
looking through that porthole of a window
across from your desk to Mount Greylock,
its blue shadows reminding you of the sea
and the freedoms you yearned for?

Whales

Ishmael was convinced whales are fish.
Of course, they aren't.
I think *you* knew they are mammals like us.
This was just one of your little jokes, wasn't it?

And when Ishmael argues that whales
will never meet the fate the buffalo suffered,
I think you are showing us his naiveté,
warning us that even these ocean beasts
could be driven to extinction.

Confess, Mr. Melville—I'm right, aren't I?

Regarding Bulkington,

Mr. Melville, if in some state of afterlife
you look down on us, are you laughing
at the scholars and readers of your masterpiece
who want to know the one exact reason
why you invested so much in Bulkington,
then buried him in chapter 23?

Did you hide him in the hold
once he had taken the tiller, guiding
the Pequod out from the sureties of land
to the insecurity of tempestuous oceans,
from the dogmatism of the lee shore
to the endless ambiguities of water?

Is he just the symbol of those who die
with their stories untold? Was he, as some say,
swept overboard by a treacherous gale?
Is he symbol of self-reliance? of freedom?
Was he a brawny modern Hercules?

Some say he was a promethean and democratic hero
you betrayed with the kiss of invisibility
because you'd finally read Shakespeare's tragedies
and devised a more flawed hero
to carry your tale to its predestined end.

Was Bulkington representative
of reason which had no role
in your allegory where free will fought
its fatal battle with the force of fate?

Or is Bulkington still in the story,
his apotheosis appearing in the spirit spout,
drawing the Pequod farther from safe shores
toward the great squid, that secret of the sea,
the *chance-like apparition of life?*

Mr. Melville, I reread these pages, suspecting
an allegorical meaning may lurk here.
I suspect you hid yourself behind his face
and name, forever restless and ready
to take to the seas of uncertainty,
rejecting the pull of rigid conventionality
and unbending belief.

Theology

Bear me out in it, thou great democratic God!
                              ~Ishmael (Chapter 26)

Great democratic God?
I ponder all that phrase may mean.
You say the democratic God
gave Bunyan the *poetic pearl*
and picked up Andrew Jackson
from the pebbles.
Was it this *democratic God*
who made Ahab captain?
Strands of fate and destiny
not woven by human hands?

And what of you, Herman?
Was it your father's failures
or the democratic *God's foot*
upon the treadle of the loom
that took you from the ranks
of the well-to-do to poverty?
Who raised you up with the popularity
of *Typee* and dropped you in the dirt
when *Moby-Dick* sank your reputation
for a century?

At the end of your book,
Ahab lies down beside the Quaker Starbuck
and Fedallah, the Parsee, beside Portuguese,
Tahitian and Maltese sailors,
the three harpooneers—African,
Gay Head Indian, South Sea Islander—,
the blacksmith, cook and carpenter,
beside Pip, the cabin boy.

All manner of men in a democratic grave.

Broken

Isn't everything broken sooner or later and sometimes
more beautiful for the cracks? We celebrate the glory of Greece
by visiting ruins, as if beauty arrives with the dust
of a tumble-down building. I doubt we'd love the Venus de Milo
as much if she were whole and perfect as when she was created.
At the Roman Baths of Caracalla, you described what remained
as *majestic & desolate grander,* admired how nature sculpted
the fallen remnants into *thousands of arches.* If you came back
and sat at your desk in Pittsfield with the text of *Moby-Dick*
on a laptop computer, deleted the encyclopedic chapter on cetology
some people hate, or edited the passages where you slipped
from Ishmael's voice to your own, I don't think we'd love
the novel as much as we do. Herman, if you hadn't been broken
by life's disappointments, would you ever have written a book?

To Herman Melville from a Generation Which Recognized Your Genius

Beginning with a line from Chapter 11

Nothing exists in itself.
Heat is not heat without cold.
Dry is but contrast to wet.
Nothing is bought that's not sold.

No evil exists without good
nor is there wrong without right.
If the sun never shone in the sky
day would not differ from night.

If the weather were always the same,
no trees would turn golden in fall
for I'm sorry, my friend, to say
that we'd have no seasons at all.

No better is there without worse.
There is no short without tall.
Nothing exists in itself;
nothing, no nothing at all.

If others refused to write
novels both large and small,
we couldn't finally declare
Moby-Dick the greatest of all.

Part IV: Backtalk—Gamming with *Moby-Dick*

Vagabond

I am tormented with an everlasting itch for things remote.
~Ishmael (Chapter 1)

I come from a long line of vagabonds.
My roots are among the uprooted
and the unrooted. My bloodstream
is a brook flowing toward the ocean;
my nerves, footpaths and caravan routes.
My ribs are railroad tracks leading
to anywhere I have not yet been.

The Flemish sailor and his Dutch wife,
the English merchant who fathered children
in Danzig, German farmers and masons
dissatisfied with their lives,
Scottish clansmen from heathered hills,
whose cousin was beheaded
outside the Tower of London,
and Huguenots exiled from France
mingled blood with Irish Catholics,
their merged generations peripatetic
on a new continent—

these wandering ancestors
bequeathed me a lust for far-off estuaries,
for untrodden paths, a desire to see
the unseen, the alien and unique.
The more different a place,
the more I am at home.

My daughter touched my hand
and craved Ireland, Australia,
bumped my foot and pined
for the Mexican Riviera, the Serengeti.
I would give her wild ponies,
saddled camels with tinkling bells,
white-water rafts.
I would give her wings and wind.
I bestow on her my nomadic blood,
my passport to the universe.

Meditation by the Water

Yes, as everyone knows, meditation and water are wedded for ever.
~Ishmael (Chapter 1)

I come to the deserted beach where dolomite cliffs
wall me off from human sounds.
Seagulls patrol the shore, squawk and scold.
Spiders skitter under rocks when I move.
This afternoon the water is gentle
as a mother's hand on the forehead
of a sick child. Reflections of hazy sun
glide tinsel-like across quiet waves—
unresolved questions, unabandoned hopes.

Another day, waves leap like panthers
after prey. Water lashes the shore.
Unfulfilled promises drip
from my battered shoulders.
When a tsunami rises from the ocean,
fleeing gulls shriek, *Why? Why? Why?*
What does the psalmist mean
when he says the Almighty will keep you
under his wings, no harm will come
to those who take refuge in God?

91

Father Mapple's Message for the 21st Century

*In this world, shipmates, sin that pays its way can travel freely, and
without a passport; whereas Virtue. . . .*

~Father Mapple (Chapter 9)

Sin that pays its way
rakes in dividends
on off-shore islands
with white sand beaches,
and unregulated banks.

Sin that pays its way
hires the best lawyers
and knows subtle means
to bribe the conscience
of a judge.

Sin that pays its way hires lobbyists
on K Street to draft legislation,
carves its large entitlements
into law while damning pitiable
payments to the poor.

Witness

I'll try a pagan friend, thought I, since Christian kindness
has proved but hollow courtesy.

~Queequeg (Chapter 10)

The bumper sticker on the car
in front of me said, *Honk*
if you love Jesus, so I did.
The driver, thinking me impatient,
gave me the finger.

After church we young adults
laughed and talked as we walked
to the Mexicana Grill for lunch.
When we finished our meal
and got our checks, some dropped
meager tips into leftover taco sauce.

The priest who preached faith
and instructed parents to raise
their children right, fondled
my friend who lit the candles
and carried the sacred chalice.

Moon Dust

For years he [the Nantucketer] knows not the land;
so that when he comes to it at last, it smells like another world,
more strangely than the moon would be to an Earthsman.

(Chapter 14)

Moon dust has no salty scent,
no fishy smell, no reminder
of brine or earthly shoreline.

It does not smell like Kansas soil
awakening in spring,
or windblown Sahara sand.

Moon dust, the dust of broken molecules
smashed by eons of meteorite collisions
left with unsatisfied electron bonds

seeking partners, has no smell at all
when left in place as it was
for billions of years, dry and destitute,

but comes alive when touched by moisture
in a lunar lander or the mucus membrane
of an astronaut's nose.

It smells something like fireplace ashes
sprinkled with water or the Indy 500,
something like spent gunpowder

but unlike the smell of land or sea
on earth, our home. We only know
from the word of astronauts

who kicked up dust, who picked up dust
on space suits, helmets and boots,
who bottled dust and brought it back

to answer questions of the curious,
their fellow sailors on this little speck
in the vast sea of space.

No Harm in Ahab?

. . . wrong not Captain Ahab, because he happens to have a wicked name.
Besides, my boy, he has a wife—not three voyages wedded—a sweet,
resigned girl. Think of that; by that sweet girl that old man has a child: hold
ye then there can be any utter, hopeless harm in Ahab? No, no, my lad;
stricken, blasted, if he be, Ahab has his humanities!
                                              ~Captain Peleg. (Chapter 16)

Can there be any hopeless harm in Robert Mugabe,
married to Grace in the *Wedding of the Century,*
her beauty and charm lighting the Kutama Mission
as the priest heard their vows? Any utter evil
in this husband and father who snubs his nose
at human rights and lets his beloved live like Marie Antoinette
at the expense of his people?

Can there be any evil in Kim Jong-Un,
who has fathered a sweet infant daughter
with his charming, soft-voiced wife?
Any tyrannous tendencies in the Supreme Leader
who eliminates those who contest his powers?

Can there be any harm in Bashar al-Assad,
loving father of three children by his wife Asma,
a beauty and builder of community centers,
who was raised and educated in London?
Can there be anything malevolent in this man
whose secret police imprison, torture and kill,
this man who bombs his own people?

Can the husbands of sweet wives, the fathers
of well-loved children become gangsters, pirates,
tyrants of ships or nations? Captain Peleg,
have you forgotten history, forgotten Herod,
Genghis Kahn, Louis XIV, Oliver Cromwell?

Elasticity

. . . see how elastic our stiff prejudices grow when love once comes to bend them.

~Ishmael (Chapter 11)

Had you known the organist who led the children's choir
in the church where I grew up, how tenderly he taught us
to sing the notes, pronounce the words, keep pace
with one another. How he laughed and teased, earning
our friendship, our desire to come each Saturday to practice
and on Sundays to sing for the congregation;

if you knew my friend, Fred, single father of four sons
after his wife died, how he worked long hours each week
to feed and clothe his boys, found time to spend with each alone
and all of them together, his loving both paternal and maternal;

had your path introduced you to Barbara, who at seventy,
still pours out love on kids in her community, devoting
hours to raising funds, planning summer programs introducing
city children to nature's riches along creek banks
and Lake Michigan's sandy shore;

or Anthony, who risks living in an impoverished neighborhood
among drugs and guns to teach work skills to teens, keeps
them too busy to join gangs, helps guide their homework
and provides fatherly love to those with no dad,
so they don't drop out of school into deep pits of despair—

yes, if you could know, really know these friends of mine,
any stiff prejudice you have against dark skin
would be elastic and begin dissolving.

Nothing

I said nothing, and tried to think nothing.
~Ishmael (Chapter 20)

I said nothing and tried to think nothing
when several boys bullied the new girl in my class,
leaving me alone for a change.

I said nothing and tried to think nothing
when one friend told a racist joke
and another belittled gays and lesbians.

When the president implied that people on food stamps
were all frauds and *welfare queens,*
I said nothing and tried to think nothing.

I said nothing and tried to think nothing
when my senator opposed legislation to keep guns
from the hands of criminals and people suffering from paranoia,

I said nothing and tried to think nothing
when refugees had their children torn from them
and sent to separate camps.

Ishmael, teach me wisdom
learned from your experience
so henceforth I will have nothing to regret.

Noah's Flood

Yea, foolish mortals, Noah's flood is not yet subsided;
two thirds of the fair world it yet covers.

(Chapter 58*)*

Two-thirds of the world is watery,
calling the vagabond, the troubled,
the adventurous, the meditative,
to come to the shore and beyond,

to sail out into the deep,
the gull and albatross overhead,
and beneath feet which play the deck like a drum,
teeming villages of dolphin, shark, squid,
and thousands of other species, many still unknown.

We've learned to love remnants
of the flood, what flows between continents
and up estuaries, waves that foam,
climb the air and fall,
the white sapphire sparkles on the surface
in moonlight or sun.

Scientists say the ice is melting,
the flood returning.
When the waters don't recede
and whole cities sink below the crest,
you and I will play the role
of Noah's neighbors.

Hosting

. . . when a black boy's host to white men with gold
upon their coats!

~Pip (Chapter 129)

I remember sit-ins and marches back in the 1960s when
northern students went south to join courageous local folk, a
small nonviolent troop sent to Mississippi to register black
citizens to vote. In those days, black men were called boys.
Black women cleaned and cooked so white women could host
dinners, fine foods served on fine china, after sending invitations to
friends and neighbors—only the right people, only white
people. Sometimes there is a turn in the lives of women and men—
a black couple in the White House hosting state dinners with
elegant women, black and white, some dressed in gold
or silver gowns. A black man as president? Pip, I swear upon
the Bible it was true. This black man's family waited upon, their
shoes polished for them, servants happily hanging their coats.

Watercolor

In that painting titled *Monster*
my friend created in ninth grade art class,
twisted harpoons jut out
of the ridged, snow-white hump
of Moby Dick like arrows
around the bullseye
of a Boy Scout archery target.

The white whale stares out from eyes
on both sides of his monstrous head,
looks both ways at once
but can see nothing coming straight on.

A lightning-strike scar
splits Ahab's sun-scorched face
from the grey hair of his hatless crown
to its hiding place beneath his grey jacket.

I imagine Ahab flinging nostalgic recollections
of young wife and son into foaming waves,
crying out, *Lower away!*
as he descends into his small boat.

His dark, monomaniacal eyes
see nothing but Moby Dick.
He will risk his life, his ship and crew
for his one purpose: vengeance
on the whale who dismasted him.

In the watercolor, Moby Dick has breached,
ripping the sea, creating colossal crests.
He has had enough of harpoons.

Survival is his goal, ridding himself
of his tormentors. His flukes
churn the water, stave the boats,
toss their crews to hungry sharks.

The white whale's massive face
with battering-ram forehead,
brow furrowed as a mountain ridge,
crooked jaw open, invites
Ahab past its ivory picket fence
into its murky cave.

The battle is drawn. I look at the title
again and ask, *Which one is the monster?*

Taking Issue with Ahab

But look ye, Starbuck, what is said in heat,
that thing unsays itself.
                    ~Ahab (Chapter 36)

Tell a child she is worthless,
will amount to nothing,
never will be truly loved,
and that poison-darted harpoon
will leave its mark.

Decades later she may drown
in a sea of alcohol, or stay
all day in her hammock,
unable to tolerate
the sunny, social deck.

If she marries a kind man,
chances are she will never believe
she deserves the proffered love.

Without thinking
of the harm she could do,
she may dart hot, sharp harpoons
into her own children's hearts.

War and Peace

Doubtless one leading reason why the world declines honoring us whalemen, is this: they think that, at best, our vocation amounts to a butchering sort of business; and that when actively engaged therein, we are surrounded by all manner of defilements. Butchers we are, that is true. But butchers, also, and butchers of the bloodiest badge have been all Martial Commanders whom the world invariably delights to honor.

~Ishmael (Chapter 24)

I walk the streets of Washington,
a city full of equestrian statues of military heroes.
I trek the full length of the Mall, pay tribute
to lost soldiers named on the black marble wall,
admire statues honoring those who fell
defending South Korea, and head
for the World War II Memorial.
I seek out the column representing Iowa,
the state from which Dad was sent
to fight for freedom overseas. Circling
the monument, I lament the deaths
of so many, the destruction of towns,
churches, museums, the many killed
in the Holocaust. I salute vets
brought to the Mall by Honor Flights.
Still, I sigh and wish there were grand monuments
to makers of peace and workers for justice.

I shuffle slowly through the split stone
representing The Mountain of Despair,
find myself standing in the shadow
of Martin Luther King, Jr. I move into a semi-circle
of stone in which are engraved the words,
It is necessary to love peace and sacrifice for it.
Heartened, I salute a man who laid his life
on the altar of peace, freedom and justice.

Tools

*To accomplish his object Ahab must use tools; and of all tools
used in the shadow of the moon, men are most apt to get out of order.*

(Chapter 46)

Here is an important truth: I am a tool or potential tool
of someone—a ship captain, politician, CEO,
the neighborhood bully, my boss. I can be played
like a violin or a kettle drum. I can be
the screwdriver turning someone else's screw,
the hammer pounding someone's nail.
It takes courage to refuse the task, resign
the commission, miss the promotion
because of protest. Too easy to be a sailor
buying into the vengeance of Ahab.
Too easy even to be the first mate, knowing
right from wrong and the risk to the whole crew,
resisting only cautiously now and then,
afraid to stand unmoving and take the consequences.
Sometimes there are only two options: to go along with evil
or *get out of order.*

Reminder

If your banker breaks, you snap; if your apothecary by mistake
sends you poison in your pills, you die.
~Ishmael (Chapter 72) Ending with a line from Chapter 13

Even here in the U.S., where Whitman,
Emerson and Thoreau wrote of individuality
and we are told to pull ourselves up
by our bootstraps, it is true:
if the housing bubble bursts, your home
is worth less than your twenty-year mortgage.
If the stock market declines, your retirement fund bleeds.

You may be the safest driver in the state,
but if the teen in the Toyota texts or drinks
and drives, you end up under carved stone.
The drive-by shooter with bad aim may miss
the Gangster Disciple and hit your daughter instead.

If your young son runs to the park
with friends, plays with the gun
Uncle Joe bought him from the Walmart toy department,
and, even if it doesn't look real, someone
in a blue uniform assumes it's loaded with lead
you have to pick a casket and plan a funeral.

Someone assassinates an archduke in Austria,
Japan bombs a U.S. naval base,
North Korea sends troops across the 38th parallel,
Iraq invades Kuwait, planes flatten the World Trade Center—
if you pause and think it through, you know Queequeg was right,
It's a mutual, joint-stock world, in all meridians.

Lamenting Fate

Here some one thrusts these cards into these old hands of mine;
swears that I must play them . . . .

~Ahab (Chapter 118)

1. In the College Adjunct Office after Teaching *Moby-Dick*

Here I am, another fall without a tenure track position.
Some days I wonder why I keep on teaching, but the
one thing I most love is to see how great literature
thrusts a torch of truth into the minds of
these students, the ones with serious intent, not the
cards who joke like Stubb in *Moby-Dick* and party their way
into academic trouble, but thoughtful collegians.
These young folks want to absorb both new and
old material. I see them in the cafeteria, their
hands holding Kindles, Nooks or open books, heads full
of ideas, expanding their worlds, ideas not just
mine or some author's now, but their own. Every good teacher
swears she can see it in their eyes, hear it in voices
that speak up in class after months of silence.
I assigned Melville's great novel again. It's a
must-read for anyone who wants to understand the
play between free will and fate. I see both of
them in my students' lives and in mine, as much as Ishmael's.

2. Behind the High School After Reading *Moby-Dick*

Don't call me no more names! I belong **here**
much as you. You're scum! I promise **some**
day you'll be sorry as hell that I'm the **one**
you picked on. Every day someone hits me or **thrusts**
a foot out to make me trip. You're mean as hell! **These**
attacks, and things you stole—my little brother's Pokémon **cards**,
my lunch money, the rotten tomatoes you stuffed **into**
my book bag, lies you told my girl about me, **these**

I can't and won't forgive. The white whale in that big **old**
book Mr. Jones made us read got his revenge. I'll get my **hands**
on you someday, drown you in a barrel **of**
boiling oil. I made this promise of **mine**
to my brother. When you beat him up, he **swears**
at me for not protecting him. Someday I'll have the courage **that**
I need to fight you. Just you wait! **I**
will some day, I swear I will. I'll be fierce! **I must**
take you bullies on and make you pay. Then I won't just **play—**
and then you'd better be with friends! You'll need **them**!

3. Nursing Home Lament after Watching *Moby-Dick*

Here is where my children choose to put me, crowded
like **some** mariner on an old whaling ship with just a hammock,
and **one** or two small spots to keep stuff in. One
nurse **thrusts** a needle in my arm with the strength of a
harpooneer. **These** things put me in a bad temper
even greeting **cards** don't dispel. Then I can't knit,
can't read or get **into** a movie. Roommates try to
cheer me up, drive **these** melancholic moods away, but I
know today I'm more **old** than I was yesterday. Just look
at my bent back, and my **hands** with bruises and visible veins.
I have almost as much **of** a limp as Ahab with his whale-bone leg.
This twisted spine of **mine** betrays me constantly.
My roommate **swears**, and on these grey days I
feel like doing **that**, too. I want a life of my own. Like Starbuck
in that movie, **I** want to go back home, but all my
children insist I **must** stay here, where everything smells like urine
and chlorine, and **play** their game. The cards thrust into our hands,
we must play **them**.

Part V: Melville

On the Wind

I have never walked the dusty trails
of Mali, the country roads
of India, but they come
to me on wings of wind.

I wipe particles of dust
from a drop-leaf table,
not knowing where they were
before they came.

The detritus of the Dust Bowl,
blown from Oklahoma,
still rides winds
around the globe.

Some say it's likely
an atom of Shakespeare,
the quintessence of dust,
has become part of my body.

Perhaps a bit of Melville
is in me, too.

Herman Melville Explains Himself

I am air
I am rain
I am hail

I am a hammer
and a nail

I mine evil

I am raven
I am eel

I am lava
I am larvae

I veil
and I reveal

Melville in Love

One version of a life, after Michael Shelden

Can love ever be wrong, he wonders,
as he wanders the Berkshire hills
with Sarah, her dark eyes melancholy
and seductive. How can it be wrong
to lean against a boulder reading
poetry to each other or rhapsodizing
on the beauty of the lake?

Can it be wrong to climb Mt. Greylock
with friends, picnic on the flat top,
drinking champagne, rum and port,
nibbling brandied cherries by the campfire
before taking Sarah's hand and disappearing
into darkness where brush and trees
seem designed to provide privacy?

He wonders again as he gallops through the country,
racing his horse against Sarah's Quake
until they call a truce, dismount by a stream
where the horses drink while he picks
black-eyed Susans for Sarah's loosened hair

as her husband minds the business in Manhattan
and his wife Elizabeth struggles through another pregnancy—
how can a relationship which brings such joy be wrong?

Phantom at Arrowhead

. . . one grand hooded phantom, like a snow hill in the air.
(Chapter 1)

I peered out the porthole of Melville's office
at Arrowhead and saw Mount Greylock
pale blue in summer light. Whale-shaped,
seeming to swim, calm in tranquil green waters
along the horizon. Nothing haunting
or horrific. Nothing malevolent.

But when winter wraps the Berkshires
in frigid air and snow sweeps in from the west,
that creature turns phantasmagoric,
a great white poltergeist. Mist rises
from the specter like the spouting
of a sperm whale, mesmerizing, menacing.

That apparition disturbed Melville's sleep,
pursued him in dreams through the dead of night
as he pursued it. Obsessed as Ahab,
he rose each day to write again about gods,
cultures, and people as changeable as the mountain,
as unpredictable and malicious as Moby Dick.

Herman Melville: Your Self-Portraits

. . . I need twenty-four self-portraits to remember who I am.
~Kilian McDonnell

At a young age, you already held together
truths of Pagan and Presbyterian, saw the limits
of each, already knew *civilized* and *cannibal*
were strands that crossed and wove themselves
into one carpet in a crumbling world
where slave could be stronger and wiser than master
and a man be honest in any skin.

You doubted the omnipotence of the gods
while affirming their beneficence.
Like Queequeg, you joined *the First Congregation
of this whole worshipping world.*

Even as you warned your readers to beware
any monomaniac who would lead the ship
of state toward ultimate disaster,
you knew anyone, even yourself,
could be pulled into the vortex of demagoguery,
join the cheers of a misguided crew.

A wanderer at heart, land scorching your feet,
you sat day after day at your desk in Arrowhead,
your pen pressed to paper, your hunt
for the white whale as obsessive as Ahab's.

Believer, doubter, melancholic, manic,
half-educated, cultured and well-read,
prophet, philosopher, writer, raconteur—
you were a pen artist, embedding self-portraits
in nearly every paragraph of your prose.

Notes

P. 17-18. An earlier version of "Ishmael in New Bedford" won first place for a Mesostic poem in the 2014 contest sponsored by the Indiana State Federation of Poetry Clubs.

P. 19. "Oceans" is a Pleiades poem. The form was invented by Craig Tigerman. Hortensia Anderson added the requirement that each line consist of six syllables.

P. 23. "The Captain" is a Spiraling Abecedarian, a form attributed to T. M. Sandrock. It could also be called a double abecedarian. Poets are allowed to use words beginning with *ex* between *w* and *y*, due to the small number of English words beginning with the letter *x*.

P. 24. "Ahab Speaks of the Wind" is an erasure poem. All the words and phrases in the poem occur in the designated chapter of *Moby-Dick,* in the order in which they are found in the poem. Sometimes an erasure poem totally changes the meaning of the passage from which it is extracted. In this case, the poem is a condensation.

P. 25. "White according to Ishmael" is an erasure poem (See "Ahab Speaks of the Wind," above, p. 24).

P. 26. "Skin, Clothes – Ishmael Shares What He Learned" is a Trimeric poem.

P. 28. "Sailor's Dreams on the Pequod" is a variation on the Asian Sonnet, a form invented by Amado Yuzon, former Poet Laureate of the Philippines.

P. 29. "Mary Starbuck's Letter" is an Abecedarian. A detailed reading of *Moby-Dick* would suggest that Starbuck is already dead by the time this letter is written because *The Bachelor* has had time to return to Nantucket. The irregular capitalization, use of the &,

etc., reflect usage in hand-written letters of the period. "Mary Starbuck's Letter" won first place in the formal poetry category of the 61st Annual Poetry Contest sponsored by Poets and Patrons in 2017.

P. 30. "Letter to Capt. Ahab from His Wife" is a Rondeau.

P. 34. "Ishmael Writes to a Friend Back Home" is a Golden Shovel poem, following the form invented by Terrance Hayes. The last words of the lines are the words of the epigraph, in order.

P. 35. "The Song of the Maltese Sailor" is a Pantoum. The chassee is a French dance.

P. 37. "Ishmael Describes Weaving with Queequeg" is an erasure poem (See "Ahab Speaks of the Wind," above, p. 24).

P. 42. "Starbuck Ponders Fate and Free Will" is a Terza Rima Variation.

P. 43. "It Wasn't a Mermaid" is a Lil Ann poem, a form created by Carrie Quick. Although the epigraph is from Chapter 4, the poem responds more directly to Chapter 126, in which the crew hears plaintive, unearthly sounds which some of them believe are mermaids.

P. 47. "Ishmael Reflects on the Try-Works Fire" is a Shakespearean sonnet. Line 1 is quoted directly from Chapter 96. The third stanza echoes the following line from Chapter 96: "The truest of all men was the Man of Sorrows, and the truest of all books is Solomon's, and Ecclesiastes is the fine hammered steel of woe. 'All is vanity.' ALL." Isaiah 53:1 refers to "the suffering servant" as "a man of sorrows, acquainted with grief" (King James Version). Christians identified Jesus as the suffering servant, and thus as the Man of Sorrows. In the 19th and early 20th centuries, most readers of *Moby-Dick* would have been aware that this title referred to Jesus. They would also have been taught that King Solomon wrote three of the books of the Hebrew Scripture (Old Testament): Proverbs,

Song of Solomon and Ecclesiastes. In this context, "Solomon's book" is most likely Ecclesiastes, the one that says "All is vanity."

P. 53. "White" is a Pleiades poem, see "Oceans," above, p. 19.

Pp. 54-55. "The White Whale Likens Himself to the Doubloon" - The doubloon is a gold coin promised to the first sailor to "call out" for Moby Dick. In Chapter 99, various crew members ponder and interpret the design on its face.

Pp. 56-57. "Stubb Ponders Shadow and Substance" is a Sestina. For the six mandatory repeated end-words, I selected six words from the epigraph. Use of homophones (as by substituting "hear" for "here" in some stanzas) is permitted.

Pp. 63-66. "Sonnet 80 Suite" is a set of poems riffing off (or dependent on) Shakespeare's 80th sonnet, a tribute to the impact reading Shakespeare's plays had on Melville's writing.

Movement 1 is a bouts sonnet using the rhyme words of Shakespeare's Sonnet 80.

Movement 2 is composed of four poems in the form called "A gram of &s." This form, created by Terrance Hayes, calls for eleven lines. The end words of each line must be words of four or more letters composed of letters in a particular word selected by the poet. Three-letter words made plural by the addition of "s" or "ed" are ruled out. The four words chosen for use in this movement (and used as titles) are all drawn from Shakespeare's Sonnet 80.

Movement 3 is a poem made up of words pulled from Shakespeare's Sonnet 80. No word is used in the poem more often than in the original sonnet

Movement 4 is an erasure poem. The words in this movement appear in the order and location on the page in which they appear in Shakespeare's Sonnet 80.

P. 67. "Lament of Queequeg's Father as Translated by an American Sea Captain" began as a villanet. The form did not provide enough space for what I wanted to say so, after the three-line stanza which normally would have been the last, I reversed the form, using the same rhyme words in reverse order. I call the result "Villanet with Reverse."

P. 79. "Boundaries" begins with three lines from "Necessities," a poem by Lisel Mueller, from her book, *Second Language* (Louisiana University Press, 1986), p. 1. The quoted words from Alexander Pope are from "Epistle to a Lady," and can be found in *The Works of Alexander Pope* (The Wordsworth Poetry Library, 1995), p. 242. Melville slightly misquotes these lines in Chapter 46 of *Omoo*.

Pp. 82-83. The first italicized phrase in "Regarding Bulkington" is from Chapter 59 of *Moby-Dick*. The second is from Chapter 90.

P. 84. The quotations in the first stanza of "Theology" are from Chapter 26. The quote in the second stanza is from Chapter 93.

P. 85. Quotes in "Broken" are from Melville's diary, as reported in "Melville in Rome, Day 3," by John Bryant: https://engjlb.wordpress.com/2014/04/03/melville-in-rome-day-3-ricordo-e-nella-cuore/, downloaded November 29, 2018.

P. 100. "Hosting" is a Golden Shovel poem (See "Ishmael Writes to a Friend Back Home", above, p. 34).

P. 105. "Tools" won first place in the Social Conscience category of the 62nd Annual Poets & Patrons Contest, 2018.

P. 107-108. Each stanza of "Lamenting Fate" represents a different voice and uses a different form, while using all the words of the epigraph. Stanza I is an Acrostic. Stanza II is a Golden Shovel (See "Ishmael Writes to a Friend Back Home," above p 34). Stanza III is a snake, a form I devised (At least I'm not aware of anyone else using this form). Here the words of the epigraph, again in order, snake their way through the poem.

P. 111. In "On the Wind," the phrase "quintessence of dust" is borrowed from Shakespeare's play, "Hamlet," Act II, Scene 2.

P. 112. "Herman Melville Explains Himself" is a Lipogram, using only letters of the alphabet in Melville's name.

P. 113. I wrote "Melville in Love" after reading Michael Sheldon's book, *Melville in Love* (HarperCollins, 2016). Shelden has convinced some scholars that Melville had an affair with Sarah Morewood; others are not convinced. Shelden considers Sarah to be the muse who inspired Melville to write a more serious novel than his earlier works. Others believe the book became more literary than it had started out to be due to Melville's friendship with Nathaniel Hawthorne and his reading of William Shakespeare's plays.

P. 115. The italicized words in Stanza 2 of "Herman Melville: Your Self-Portraits" are quoted from Chapter 13 of *Moby-Dick*.

About the Author

Wilda Morris's grandmother and mother taught her to love poetry. She became serious about writing poetry after the death of her first grandchild.

Wilda has served as president of both the Illinois State Poetry Society and Poets & Patrons, a Chicago poetry organization for which she continues to serve as Workshop Chairperson. She has led poetry workshops for children and for adults. For several years, she was on the staff of the Christian Writers' Conference at the Green Lake Conference Center in Wisconsin. She has also led workshops in Illinois and Iowa.

Wilda's first book, *Szechwan Shrimp and Fortune Cookies: Poems from a Chinese Restaurant,* was published by RWG Press in 2008. Another poetry manuscript, *The Unapproved Uncle,* will be looking for a publisher soon. Wilda has published widely in journals, websites, newspapers, and anthologies, and has won awards for formal poetry, free verse and haiku. *Wilda Morris's Poetry Challenge* at wildamorris.blogspot.com provides a contest for other poets each month.

Wilda is a graduate of American University and the University of Illinois. She also has an M.Div.

Made in the USA
Columbia, SC
23 February 2019